The poems in this anthology have been selected from ForcesPoetry.com – a website created for all poets, including members of the Armed Forces and their families.

Forces Poetry is part of the Forces Literary Organisation Worldwide (FLOW FOR ALL) which is dedicated to offering assistance to those who have suffered from the effects of war, especially the suffering shared by servicemen and women, their relatives and their friends.

Proceeds from the sale of this book will be used to support the work of FLOW FOR ALL, helping them to become a registered charity and to employ counsellors for those in need of care and support.

For more information please visit the following websites:
flowforall.org
forcespoetry.com
forcesstories.com

Published in paperback by Silverwood Books 2008
www.silverwoodbooks.co.uk

ISBN 978-1-906236-07-6

British Library Cataloguing in Publication Data
A CIP catalogue record for this book is available from the British Library

Set in 11pt Bembo by SilverWood Books
Printed in England on FSC Accredited woodfree paper by Biddles Ltd

® **Mixed Sources**
Product group from well-managed
forests, controlled sources and
recycled wood or fiber
www.fsc.org Cert no. TT-COC-002303
© 1996 Forest Stewardship Council
FSC

Voices of the Poppies

an anthology

by

Forces Poetry

The poems appear as they were submitted by the poets,
uncensored and without correction.

Some poems may be considered graphic in nature
and therefore unsuitable for younger readers.

These have been marked **Content Caution**.

CONTENTS

Vera Lynn DBE

Vera Lynn DBE

Through my own experiences in talking with the boys and girls about their thoughts on war and how they felt about going into action, many would just shrug.

'It's what we are trained to do,' they would say.

For most their thoughts are so personal, and even for the most articulate often difficult to put into words without aggrandizement. Yet through poetry they express themselves with absolute clarity, deep feeling and simplicity. I only have to read the poem *In Flanders Fields* by Lt Col John McCrae or Kipling's *Tommy* to fully appreciate and be thankful for the beauty of Forces Poetry.

To see this tradition still flourishing in the fertile minds of today's young men and women of our armed forces is gratifying and humbling. They leave us such a precious legacy which is matched by their courage, honour and duty.

We must never forget them.

Yours

Vera Lynn

.

Deborah Tainsh

Mother of Sergeant Patrick Tainsh, who gave his life in the service of his country.

On February 12 2004 at 6 am, before the sun pierced the darkness, a knock exploded against the front door. Outside stood two US soldiers dressed in class A's. We knew the reason instantly. Our son had been killed in Iraq.

That moment changed our lives forever and cast us into a 'new norm' that many families across the globe have become a part of. We are the families of military men and women who have died in the 21st century's new wars on terrorism in Afghanistan, Iraq, and other areas around the world. Our time has come to pay for freedom through the sacrifice of our own.

After Patrick's death, emotions unlike any ever experienced enveloped us. Faith collapsed in the questioning of why our prayers weren't answered. Verbal communications went on lock-down with no way to express to each other what we were going through. There was no one to validate the darkness and fog we walked in and whether or not we would survive it.

As I lost interest and the feeling of unity with others through activities that I had previously had a passion for, I delved into solitude and writing. I had to write for fear of forgetting Patrick, his movements, his voice, his smile, his humor. I had to write to validate his existence. I had to write to release the grief, pain, anger, and to acknowledge that our son was really dead... I also had to write so that Patrick's legacy would live on and his life would serve others, even beyond death. As the world continues to meet new challenges and sacrifices, the words from the hearts and minds of its poets and writers will remain to leave behind footprints of our time here.

My greatest hope is that these footprints in the form of the poetry in this Forces Poetry anthology will help others to see, feel, taste, and touch the experiences of our current journeys, to find the most beautiful memories in the darkest moments and to heal from the deepest wounds.

Deborah Tainsh, USA
Author of Heart of a Hawk: One family's sacrifice and journey toward healing
www.heartofahawk.com

Graham Knight

Father of Sgt Benjamin James Knight, who gave his life in the service of his country

Ben's Mum and I have cried every day since his death. I don't think we will ever come to terms with losing our youngest son in Afghanistan, in the Nimrod Crash on 2nd September 2006. Andrew and Matthew, his brothers, miss him terribly. Ben was so full of life; he always made us laugh and had an unquenchable thirst for adventure. He was kind and loving and would put others before himself.

Sergeant Benjamin James Knight was 25 years old when he was killed, and we are thankful and very proud to have spent those years with him. He believed in the job he was doing, helping to free the Afghan people from what is seen as the tyranny of the Taliban regime. He wanted them to enjoy the freedom that we in the West expect and all too often take for granted.

It is vital that we continue to support our servicemen and woman – when they are sent to various conflicts, when they come home from them and in later years after their service has ended. Without their courage and bravery the world would be a much darker place.

I wrote my poem through a veil of tears and read it out at Ben's funeral. The act of putting my thoughts into writing somehow helped me to move on a few steps. I only hope that people reading this book of poems and the poems on the Forces Poetry website will gain an insight into the sacrifices that our boys and girls and their families have made.

Graham Knight
A very proud but sad Dad
www.benknight.co.uk

SOLDIERS PRAYERS

Brave soldier we are so proud of you
Your country cannot ask for more
You've made the ultimate sacrifice
Now you're knocking on Heaven's door

Rest in peace brave soldier
You served Queen and country well
The Lord above is calling you
You're free at last, from hell

It's time for you to take your place
Among those soldiers who passed over before
For like them you're now a star in the skies up above
Shining down on earth forever more

Brave soldier you'll never be forgotten
Know that your family still love you and care
And you'll stay in the hearts of your brother's in arms
So your memory will always be there

We will not say goodbye to you Soldier
But rather 'See you soon'
For one day we will join you up there
In those stars above the moon

So let the Angels guide you
To the 'special' stars above
To your final resting place
Where you can rest in peace with God's love

Michaela Turner

IN THE TRENCH

I sit cold, damp and wet
Tasting the smell of the crackling guns.
I am waiting for the signal
To hop over the trench
I am scared and nervous.

I can hear the signal
I am terrified and thinking of home.
My children's lovely hugs
The smell of warm fresh bread
A frothy beer with all my friends.

And now I am here
In Flanders fields
Blood red poppies grow
Around my grave
I missed my home very much
But now I can never go back.

Alice Walker (Age 9)

A CRY FOR HELP

Some years ago a cry was heard
A cry for help from far away
So we shoulderd arms and packed our bags
Ne'er a questioning word did we say.

To airport,dockside,by bus and train
loved ones wept and waved goodbye
Eyes front! dont look back
Least we see yon watered eye.

Rifle cleaned and stowed away
kitbag full to burstin'
Tropic lands await us
Damp and wet and steamy

No question of what we do
We're here to help Malaya
Rid them of the Commie bastards
Show 'em what we're made of.

When job were done and home we went
To welcome arms we left behind
We'd sit and chat and sleep in peace
Expecting nowt from you our friend.

A medal struck such a shock
what for? we ask in deep suprise
for helping us in time of need
wear it on yer chest wi' pride

The Queen says yes lads its ok
the MOD say different!
I'll wear it Ma-am cos its mine
The MOD can go where the sun dont shine.

Gordon Smith

Less We Forget

The old man in the corner who stares into space
The story of time etched on the lines on his face
He sits there and remembers those to the left and his right
The soldiers and friends who had gone to the fight

He remembers the cold and the dirt and the smells
He remembers his mates who were wounded and fell
The cold of the night and the heat of the day
The fields full of Poppies where his friends fell and lay

The old man sits alone with his memories and drink
A time to remember, to remember and think
He thinks of the good times as well as the bad
He thinks of the life, the friendship he has had

People look over and see the man on his own
They wonder why this old feller sits their all alone
If they asked him he'd tell them I'm here with my friends
I spend it with them on every Remembrance weekend

So I'm not sitting here all alone and depressed
Cos I share my time here with the bold and the best
The blokes who stood fast and who answered the call
They are always beside me, still young one and all

The old man sups up and he heads for the door
He ventures outside to the memorial once more
To stand and pay tribute and his respects he does send
And to stand beside others who remember their friends

Remembrance Sunday, less we forget
Is a chance to remember, a chance to respect
A chance to remember we promised and said
A chance to remember the Glorious Dead

So when you see these old soldiers just sitting in the bar
Pull a chair up beside them and the chances are
They will share a few drinks and a story or two
Of the men who bought freedom for me and for you

Chris Dickson

This Mask We Wear

Look under the mask we soldiers wear,
look under the mask if you dare.
Look under the mask and see behind,
Or are you scared of what you'll find.

We are not beasts nor men of war,
we do not wait to hear deaths door.
We do not relish the death we see,
we only fight by your decree.

You condemn us all as if you knew,
you say your words without a clue.
You dare not look into our eyes,
dying daily under scorching skies.

We serve and watch our brother's fall,
but hear the names you give us all.
Please take a moment look and see,
our fears, our terror, our misery.

We are not heroes from comic books,
we're not all handsome blessed with looks.
We are not fearless men of war,
but merely reapers by deaths door.

You sent us here or so it seems,
and expect our hands to stay so clean.
But in this place we see such sights,
which make your sons change overnight.

You hear of a child just last night killed,
and the fathers heart with hatred filled.
You say god bless please don't feel shame,
if I were he I'd feel the same.

But in our case you blame us quick,
no thought of what has made us sick.
It was not daughter, son or kin,
but one of our brothers – our brethren.

We really are a band of brothers,
our mates beside us from one mother.
She guides us through both day and night,
and if we're lucky past the fire fight.

And when a son of hers doth die,
in writhing agony screaming why.
His brothers gathered by his side,
we hold his hand and watch him die.

You have to know just how this felt,
my brother a boy (God how I wept).
He squeezed my hand and kissed it too,
and begged for me to pull him through.

I lied of course and told him "sure",
I lied because there was no cure.
I lied to let him die in peace,
I lied to make his pleading cease.

We watched him crying, spewing blood,
we watched him twitching soaked in mud.
We held him tight to let him know,
his brothers were with him – time to go.

To go through this but not just then,
but time and time more boys again.
You tend to lose the human code,
and mutate into killing mode.

Are we still human I hear you ask,
it changes daily from task to task.
But picture now what we go through,
now ask yourself the truth, could you?

I am not here to change the bad,
what some do in war is more than sad.
But try to imagine the awful facts,
you can't get close, thank God for that.

Your little boy who went to war,
your little baby to foreign shores.
Please understand we still are here,
but look past our sin and see our tears.

We've seen such horrors done to mates,
we've lain and wept till sleep us takes.
Our nightly dreams of things gone past,
bodies of others torn by blasts.

So when you condemn our brothers now,
Remember please this poem and how –
We've paid for war with blood and sin,
please don't make us pay yet again.

But if you want to hound us down,
bring us to justice before the crown.
Bear this in mind before you do,
what would you have done if we were you?

I'd not have done it I hear you shout,
they signed the line let's throw them out!
God help you sleep at peace tonight,
and pray you never have to fight.

To close this poem I admit the shame,
the guilt of sin this weight of pain.
I'll live with this my whole life through,
give thanks to God it was not you.

Like soldiers gone in wars before – adieu.

The Sandman

A Soldiers Wish

I walked into the NAAFI bar, I saw them all around
The youngest of them bladdered by the beer that he had downed
I walked about from group to group listening to their chat
They talked about the old days with Danny Bill and Pat

I took a seat and leaned right back I felt the saddened air
I felt their sorrow oozing from the roots of every hair
I sat and listened to them all, I laughed at all their tales
I sat and watched them laughing as they drank their many ales

I watched them all that afternoon like any father would
I saw the boss come in for one not just because he should
He joined the lads to show respect as he's done before
To say goodbye to those he loved killed in bloody war

He stood their proudly saying his words, he really did us proud
He talked about their Sergeant with a pint up on his cloud
We gave three cheers we wiped the tears we even hugged a little
The daily fight of life and death out here is very brittle

Then wisely he said to them come on lads that's enough
If he were here right now he'd say "enough's a bloody nough"
How right he was indeed I would have said that very phrase
I was always glad we had a boss who everybody praised

One by one they left the bar, the gathering was done
I got to my feet and headed out into that burning sun
And as I ducked outside the door I went to stand up straight
But standing there in front of me was Billy my best mate.

He stood there staring straight at me as if he saw me there
Then in a voice so soft and proud he said to me with care
They loved you mate just like a dad, just like their own at home
We "never" will forget you, wherever we may roam.

I stood there in dumb silence, I couldn't say a word
I felt the tears come surging and soon my eyes were blurred
Cos stopping momentarily with one last teary look
He gave the finest tribute, a beautiful salute

I watched Bill walk away right then and called my god to me
I gave my thanks and asked him for a final sight to see
He said "if one wish I give to you, what then would it be"
"No more wars" I said to him "until eternity"

"For Connor"
Mac Macdonald

Let Me Lie

Let me lie with my comrades who were lost in the war
Let me lie in peace overlooking this remote shore
Let me lie with my comrades in this plot so small
Let me lie with those who will never age at all

Remember my comrades in the cold dark sea
Remember those who have no headstone to see
Let me lie with my comrades in this land far away
Let me lie while you pray that the World will be at peace
one day

The Falklands War
1982
Peter Southern

Daddy's Gone

I have to tell them Daddy's gone
Their faces smiling how they shone
I looked around their room to see
The gifts they made for their Daddy

I feel the pain begin to swell
The pain of death that comes from hell
I feel the tears well up again
That pain that makes us go insane

I sit them down to let them know
their bestest Daddy had to go
I say my words and feel them shake
their hearts oh god I heard them break

Daddy's girls have lost their glow
The saddest news they both now know
The sobbing starts and never ceases
Night after night their hearts in pieces

When they asked me why this is
I hold them tight and give each a kiss
I'm sorry darlings is all I say
I only know he's gone away

Inside my soul I know much more
How daddy was killed in another's war
How he hated killing other fathers
On orders from political masters

If I could punish politicians
I'd send them on the cruellest mission
To sit with children just like mine
And face an orphans question time

"For my Girls"
Annie

THE DET

Alone in the corner,
The Irish music blaring.
Don't look up, don't look round,
The I.R.A. are staring.

Have they sussed me ? Shall I leave ?
A long way to the door.
Oh God ! I feel them coming,
Slowly cross the floor.

With shaking hands, I raise my eyes,
They stare into my face.
"You spying English bast★★★!"
My heart begins to race

I think of torture, will I cope?
A black sack on my head.
Will I scream, as they begin?
I could be home in bed.

I asked for this detachment,
I shouldn't really moan.
At it now for six full month,
My mind it dreams of home.

They walk on past, so close to feel.
The wee runs down my leg.
The fear released inside me.
I down my final dreg

At the table right behind me,
Sits back-up Dave, my mate.
It wasn't me they wanted !
It's Dave, it's him, it's fate !

I want to leave, I want to run,
Escape here whilst I can.
How can I leave him all alone ?
Desert another man ?

My Browning's in my trousers,
Thirteen rounds in all.
How many could I "Take out"?
Before my final fall ?
"Save him now!" a voice screams out,
The voice inside my head.
Why risk myself as well ?
When Dave's as good as dead.

I turn away, avert my eyes,
My luck is in this night.
I catch a glimpse of begging eyes,
He's got no chance to fight.

They march him past me, held so tight,
Dave's legs have gone to jelly.
They drag him out the back door,
A lane, so dark and smelly.

The crowd pours out, I'm sucked along,
In to the pouring rain.
Dave is down upon his knees,
His face so full of pain.

He looks at me, a silent prayer,
"You'd help me if you could"
The sack goes down upon his head,
I will ! I can't ! I should !

I stand there weeping silent tears,
So helpless do I feel.
Why die along beside you ?
Don't ask me as you kneel !

The pistol rests against Dave's head
The gunman looks right at me
Does he know I'm one of them ?
"I'm not ! I'm Irish ! See ?

I slide my hand inside my belt,
The metal of the gun feels cold.
But I know that I won't use it,
To die before I'm old!

The crowd all give "The Thumbs-down",
The signal to shoot.
My thumb it goes down with them,
I'm staring at my boot

The killer laughs right at me,
His finger on the trigger.
I'm sure he knows, I'm one of them,
He shoots ! A silent snigger.

Graffiti grows upon the wall,
Mingled with the rain.
A closer look, not chalk, not paint,
Just bits of poor Dave's brain

I walk away down cobbled lane,
The killer shouts a warning !
"Don't come back upon our turf, !
You'd die before the morning ! "

They've let me go, tonight I live,
With the I.R.A., no messing.
To live with what I did to Dave,
"Go home and learn a lesson!"

I often think about that night,
And if I could've saved him.
Would Dave forgive me if he knew ?
I've since risked life and limb

Was I a coward long ago ?
Or was I only Human ?
To save myself, at his demise,
I bet he's bloody fuming !

A time long ago, over the water

Tom Mcgreevy

ABSOLUTION

My fingers are torn and bleeding
My skin has shrunk to my bones
I have no strength, such is my hunger
Starvation is cruel and unyielding
And the cold, always the cold
Their is no heat here in Ho8
'The tunnels below the earth'.
I swing my pick axe, and a
Small piece of rock falls at my feet
It is not enough; they are angry
The blows from their sticks
Fall upon my shoulders
I tell myself I am immune!
But I am not, and it hurts
I feel unbearable pain
Would my mama recognise me now?
The once proud son she bore?
I think not; I cry out for her
Mama, mama! And they beat me once more.
Close by an explosion echoes
Showering us in red sandstone dust
Now we are not so different
Brothers; eyes locked in fear
For they have a mama too.

The heavy sound of footsteps
Cuts into the moment; they are panicking
I am hauled to my feet
And forced to join the slow moving ranks
Of the lost souls of men
Slaves of the German Third Reich
Leaving their dead behind.
The passage is long and the way unstable
An old man slips and falls
Amongst the polished boots
Desperately his fingers clasp my ankle
He calls to me 'Comrade, I beg of you'
I ignore him and shake him free
In my single-mindedness to reach the light.
Oh! Such bitter sweet relief
To taste the sweet, sweet air
I close my eyes and am lost in its freedom
My mind elsewhere; I see papa!
Working the land of my birth
But no; it is the old man that is there!
Oh my papa! My papa! Forgive me!
I couldn't help him! Dear God, I couldn't help him!
And as the evening sky descends upon me
I fall to my knees in repentance
My darkness is absolute.

Jan Hedger

Footnote: This poem is for all those who suffered, and for those who lost their lives in the construction of the Hohlsgangsanlagen *– what we know today as The Jersey War Tunnels/Underground Hospital – during the German occupation of the Channel Islands.*

Pit Ponies And Fireflys

I crept out of bed quietly, when the house was asleep,
Then out the back door, and up into my tree ,
This was the way to watch the fireflies display.
I settled down to creep into the lives of those not sleeping.
The screech of a vixen, like a maiden in terror.
Such a strange way to summon a lover,
But it must be the strongest to make her a mother .

It was then that I saw them, on the brow of the hill,
Dark shapes of such beauty, in black silhouette,
the proud black stallion, long main flowing.
Maybe a hundred ponies, the young and the old,
So wild, so free, going to rest in some secret place,
The scene so intense ,the fireflies forgotten.
They could not match the spectacular sight,
Of so many ponies tossing their heads in the night.

I dawdled to school one morning later, still thinking,
And scheming how to observe without causing fright,
Those graceful coal black creatures i saw in the night.
Then I heard shouting and cracking of whips,
And the sound of unshod hooves, on hard tarmac tapping.
Then they came into sight, and in place of their leader
Rode a man on a horse, demanding they follow,
with two more behind, whistling and shouting,
Lashing their whips from left and to right,
Eyes glaring, nostrils flaring. Open mouths frothing,
Bodies all flecked with their sweat and spittle,
I drew back in horror as they passed in terrified flight,
Could these be the beautiful creatures I had seen in the night?

Rounded up, herded into pens they waited,
Listening to the clank of shunted cattle trucks.
The weaker ones stood, heads bowed in defeat,
But a few raised theirs high, to neigh defiance.

All longed for the freedom of firefly hill,
but they were now part of a humans cash crop.
I stayed with them for all of that morning,
School boys are right to rebel when they see grief,
For those sweet creatures were doomed, some to go blind,
Deep in the earth, where man and horse mined.

That night as I watched, the fireflies flitted,
They did not excite me, I wanted to see
that proud black stallion with all that remained
of his large family, still running wild and free.
I never saw him again, but I heard him that night.
His snorting stamping and anxious whinnies.
His neighing drifted down on the darkness it stirred,
As he searched in vain for the rest of his herd.

Now as I grow older, I still think of them,
Deep underground in the stale air and dust.
Do they still think of their sweet life on the hill,
when they see the lights on human heads nodding,
As they toil together, the fireflies mocking.?
And is that the sound of a Vixen's screech,
Or the scream of a human under a rock fall.?
There are no winners in this underground hell.
Where day means night, and all day all night.
Does some kind collier with work worn hands
gently wash off the dust and the grime,
To let them breathe freer and see just a bit.?
Think kindly of me as you leave me behind.
For I cannot help you, except in my mind.

A. R. Lewis

An Angel Came To Visit Today

An angel came to visit today
On this day I now know why
I swear I could hear her cry

As I patrolled down the streets
My maker the players did want me to meet
The war was on
A soul was to be moved on

A loud bang and a flash
No time to dash
I end up covered in rubble rash
I cough and splutter
I hope they catch the nutter

As I lay there and look up to the sky
No tears left inside me I cannot cry
My angel she looks down on me
No words are spoken her silence is not broken
Her hand outstretched all warm and glowing
We both are knowing its time to be going

As I rise over the land
Still holding my angels hand
I look down and see… ME
My mates are a flutter they want to kill some nutter
But I am at peace I feel no hate or urge to go out and hurt

I look into her eyes
This time I do cry
My angel breaks her silence and she asks me why do I cry
I did not get a chance to say goodbye
So that is why I cry

I see the light at the end of the tunnel
I look to my angel
She smiles and let's go of my hand
This journey is not finished
Walk into the light
And please do not take fright
For you my friend must walk into the light

John Sinclair

To Ben

You took to the sky that fateful day, full of life and joy,
You took to the sky that day, our brave boy
You didn't know it was your last, so your banter was the same
The crew all working hard, as more height you gained.

Our lovely boy, so high above a country far away
Our lovely boy, our Ben our son we sadly lost that day.
Our Ben, our precious youngest son so lively full of fun
He was so loved by all of us, it's hard to think he's gone

Ben was like a little brother all his friends agree
The best friend you could have, they have said to me
There was only one Ben Knight, he was unique you see
There will never be another Ben not for you or me

We shall always remember you Ben, in every little way
We will never forget you Ben, not even for a day.
We loved you Ben we told you so, you said you loved us too
We want to put our arms around you, that's all we want to do

But go you must, you have been called to fly with Angels now
So night, night Ben you sleep well our heads we will bow.
One day perhaps we'll meet again in a land so far away
Once more to talk and laugh with you, I look forward to that day.

Graham Knight

My Daddy

I love you
Lots and lots
You love me too
Dad you are the nicest
Dad in the world
How I love you
Lots and lots

Amy (Aged 7)

THE RAINFOREST STORY

I remember when life was sweet.
I danced with gorgeous tropical flowers on my body,
Like a great army of trees.
I sang with the sweet, colourful parrots.
Life was sweet; life is forgotten.

A time before awful machines came.
Before fiery chainsaws were made to haunt me.
Now all that is left is the remains of trees,
And rotten leaves and old tropical fruits,
That the animals ate before they fled.

Children! Come and find me.
For I am your inheritance.

Poppy Slevin (Age 10)

CONNOR

Colder now the nights draw in
No more scran from your mess tin
No more worry you may have sinned
No more moving like the wind

Older now I have become
with memories of pain and fun
But brightest yet my time with you
I wish these times we could renew

Not to weep I know you'd say
Live your life to the full each day
Get a grip I hear you call
Why did God let my brother fall?

Never perfect we said we were
Our parties held so we'd deter
All forms of terror we swore to rid
"Stand by Stand by" you me and Sid

Over and over I hear your words
That laugh so wicked you'd scare the birds
But underneath your armoured vest
You were my brother, the bloody best

Rendezvous with all our mates
Grab each hand and for me shake
I leave you now to meet your keeper
I'll catch you later when I greet the reaper

The old git ROATS

How Far To Lashkar Gah?
(The voice of politics speaks to the voice of caution)

How far is it to Lashkar Gah,
To Helmund's vale and Kandahar?
There where two pleasant rivers flow,
And groves of pomegranate grow?

Too far, too far. One thousand years,
Along a road of bitter tears.
Through bloody crimson poppy fields.
And evil is the crop it yields.

So we shall send a NATO force,
To guide them on a better course.
There is a plan; we have a scheme,
"Provincial Reconstruction Team."

And while you're building twelve new schools,
The shadow-men, who know no rules,
Through fear, and not the rule of law,
Have closed one hundred twenty more.

Oh cynic you! Is it not strange,
How people there all pray for change?
And with us wish to build and learn,
So with God's will, the tide will turn.

One thousand years, in peace and grace,
The Sultans ruled that fertile place.
Then Mongols came one fearsome day,
And they imposed a "better" way.

But they brought fierce and savage days,
Of tribal feuds and war-lords ways,
How can such tales, so far away,
Have bearings on our plans today?

From Ghengis Khan to Tamerlane.
Through Ahmed Shah Durrani's reign.
With British intervention thrice.
Who set the cost? Who paid the price?

Ours is a democratic voice,
We act upon the peoples' choice.
The cost? The price? Part of the game!
And what we do, is in your name.

Can you recall the "Hill of Bones"?
And General Burns and Elphinstones?
When Akbar Khan so gravely lied,
And sixteen thousand British died.

But that was born of treachery
And lack of skills in soldiery
This time we have good faith, and trust
And all will see our cause is just.
Four decades on, close to Maiwand
A thousand soldiers of our land,
Were killed by Afghans in one day.
Please learn from this. Or learn to pray!

Forget the spectres of the past.
For we shall go, the die is cast.
Morale is high, our troops fear naught,
And all deserve our best support.

I could not grudge our troops goodwill.
I pray them well and free from ill.
Come home each one from Kandahar.
God keep you safe in Lashkar Gah

Paddy Slevin

IN REMEMBRANCE OF AMANDA
1985-2007

CLOUDS

Clouds
Are a patchwork blanket
Where angels sit having a picnic
Are they big balls of cotton wool or candyfloss
Is someone hiding among the clouds
Sometimes they get angry and cry.
Maybe they can see what we are
Doing to our world

Amanda Rapley-Redfern (Age 14)
St Piers, Lingfield, UK

THE PANSY

inside the pansy a new universe,
the ladybird chases aphid
through petals and stalks to the edge of the world.
dewdrops like stars
catch the ladybirds eye,
stargazing in awe at the night sky.
me and the lady bird sit together in the garden,
contemplating the universe beyond the pansy.

From Amanda's sketchbook,
Submitted by Jan Hedger

WHY

I've walked the leafy lanes of England.
Climbed the daunting mountains of Wales.
I've sat cramped in Irish darkness,
whilst my Scot's blood boiled.

I've lived like a cowboy, on the north American plains.
Drank for tomorrow, and the day after that.
I've listened to the rain as it crashed on tropical trees.
Tipped sand from my boots, while the sun browned my knees.

No shit, that's the motto.
No dead, no wounded.
Jungle rules apply.
Duty fighter front and centre.

Not for flags.
Nor Kings.
Not for Queen nor country.
It's for your mates.

James Love

My Dad At Sea

Midnight sky turns to blue,
I hate the days I'm away from you,
Days go by,
That I can't stop the urge to cry,
I hate the days I'm away from you,
The days are long,
While you're away everything goes wrong,
I hate the days I'm away from you,
The longer you're away the less I can fight it,
And I just sit and try to drown it,
I hate the days I'm away from you,
Every day midnight sky turns to blue,
And the navy tries to destroy the love I have for you.

For my dad, who is out at sea
Connor McInnis (Age 13)

MY SERGEANT MAJOR

Here comes the sergeant major
If he sees that beer he'll take it
He ain't a one to mess with
As he shouts "you little …

Git he called me last time
You could tell that he was plastered
He said I read your records laddie
So I know that you're a …

Mastered skills like shooting
He's done his time and how
But he's got an awful tongue
As he called his wife a …

Now that we are off to war
He's given us all some succour
But even now he loses it
And says "you little …

Tucker said he likes him
He says he's strong and bright
Sarnt major don't like Tucker
cos he said he's full of …

Dite deft dite he screams at us
Of that I'm truly sick
He shouts and screams all day at us
I think the mans a …

Mick and I had drinks to serve
to the officers (ex rankers)
To sum up sergeant majors
They're all a bunch of …

Jankers now he's given me
As in the mess he frollicks
I hope the war dogs find him
and bite him in the bollocks

Sandy

The Futility Of War

Men and women go to war
To fight another lands cause
Sent by those who have never been
Those who can't imagine
The things these soldiers see or do

Bullets fly, bombs fall, Star-shell's flare
Novices cautioned for peering over the parapet
Beyond the wire, stained with blood to rust, into No Man's
Land.
Soldiers die, children cry, still they have to be strong,
Have to carry on, as if nothing is wrong

The soldiers - mothers, wives, fathers and sons,
Don't always miss the bullets fired at them
Soldiers sent home injured or dead
Only to find no support for the broken
Never to be the same person they were before.

Bugler playing, tears streaming
Soldiers stand tall and straight,
Wounded inside and out
Feel the pain, loneliness, loss of hope,
Sharing the same nightmares –
Day and night
Yet another comrade
Laid to rest.

Anna Bartlett

Think

Think of all the men
Who died for you and me
Who were all out there when
We were having tea

Think of how they felt
Going out to war
Think of how they must have knelt
To pray before the lord

Out to save their country
They knew what they had to do
Ready to carry out their duty
To save me and you

A roar of guns, a clash of thunder
They fixed their bayonets
Many of our troops fell asunder
Many men regret

There that day
Our men did lay
In the Flanders Fields
The poppies rose
To commemorate
The caring men who fell

Ruby (Age 11)

Last Of The Few

The young man spun his wheels again,
And black smoke rose like soot,
For 1600 big CCs,
Lay waiting 'neath his foot.

The young lad grinned at the old man,
Who'd never know the thrill,
Of a head to head on the 229,
Or a ton down Bluebell Hill.

The old man grinned right back at him,
For the lad brought back a face,
Of another boy from long ago,
Who lost a different race.

My motor was a Merlin Rolls,
I played the deadly game,
For in my wings were Brownings eight,
And Hurricane its name.

I see it now, that summer's day,
It dawned so bright and fair,
And as the call to scramble came,
I said my daily prayer.

Is this, Dear Lord, to be the day,
To be my day of fate,
And will it be by 109,
Or Junkers eighty-eight?

And as we climbed the burning blue,
Eyes straining for the Hun,
The 109s were quick that day,
The odds, twenty to one.

Young Jimmy turned and dived away,
His throttle thru' the gate,
A Messerschmitt hot on his tail,
Intent to seal his fate.

The Merlin screamed his last lament,
From fifteen thousand down,
Into a Sussex hillside,
His grave was never found.

Best spin your wheels my Lovely Lad,
And make the old folks frown,
Than walk your girl down Hitler Strasse,
In the heart of London Town.

15/09/2003
Roland Gardner
Husband of Sally Gardner

STORMIN' NORMAN
A tribute to 'General H. Norman Schwarzkopf'

The Kuwait Invasion
In 1990 Saddam, the gangster knave...
The monster from Mesopotamia... the maniac...
Did Kuwait's dominion and oil wealth crave.
But his invasion would soon be driven back.
For the thief of Baghdad made an enormous blunder...
While Norman prepared for Instant Thunder.

Refrain

Saddam Hussein did misbehave...
When through Kuwait his troops went swarmin'.
But the thief of Baghdad could only rant and rave...
When Stormin' Norman did the performin'.

Desert Shield

In that late summer... by September...
Norman's first plan was then revealed.
A great coalition he would form...
For the Operation Desert Shield.
The pilferer dithered and held back the throttle...
The monster had truly lost his bottle.

Refrain

Saddam Hussein did misbehave...
When through Kuwait his troops went swarmin'.
But the thief of Baghdad could only rant and rave...
When Stormin' Norman did the performin'.

Desert Storm

The storm sent airmen off on high…
The Baghdad bully's force to wreck.
The allied angels filled the sky…
And on the ground caused great havoc.

Soon the dictator's ill conceived plans
Were buried in the desert's sands.

Refrain

Saddam Hussein did misbehave…
When through Kuwait his troops went swarmin'.
But the thief of Baghdad could only rant and rave…
When Stormin' Norman did the performin'.

Desert Sword

The coalition fought shoulder to shoulder…
And unleashed the power of the Sabre,
Their great advance grew bolder and bolder…
As the Republican Guard they did belabour.
From allied armour the mob had shied…
They fled bewildered and terrified.

Refrain

Saddam Hussein did misbehave…
When through Kuwait his troops went swarmin'.
But the thief of Baghdad could only rant and rave…
When Stormin' Norman did the performin'.

Aftermath

Norman you truly are a hero warrior…
To the Saudis… to Britain and the United States.

Great indeed is your leadership… but greater
Is the debt owed and the gratitude of Kuwait's.
It leaves only one thing for me to say…
We all should have a national 'Norman' Holiday.

Refrain

Saddam Hussein did misbehave…
When through Kuwait his troops went swarmin'.
But the thief of Baghdad could only rant and rave…
When Stormin' Norman did the performin'.

2007
Kevin M Welsh

Thanks To You

I had some painful memories of a time I'd left behind
I saw some awful things out there still pictured in my mind
I had no wish to carry on it all seemed too much grief
but with love and perseverance you gave me self belief

I will never lose my demons no matter what I do
But now I see the lighter colours coming through from you
I know that it's been difficult to help a wreck like me
But thanks to you I live my life with less uncertainty

I hurt you so much earlier I didn't mean to do it
we seem to hurt those closest, those who help us through it
Only when I saw you crying I felt so bad inside
When I said I hated you please believe I lied

You put up with my shouting my constant lack of life
But now I thank the god upstairs for making you my wife
So what I say to all of you who feel as I did then
Don't forget the life you had – get it back again

Perfect it may never be, those demons still will lurk
But chat and conversation will help to ease the hurt
Love the ones you have with you, and children even more
And thank your god you have them to love and to adore

For Helen
Andy

THE GHOSTS OF BRIDGNORTH

As I wandered down a tree lined road
just a way from Bridgnorth town
I remembered lads in airforce blue
smartly marching up and down

I can see the concrete patches
where all the wooden huts once stood
and recall the cold dark winter days
out there gathering coke and wood

I can still hear voices shouting
the click of heels upon the ground
the shouts of 'Alt, "Stand Still" "You plonker"
then silence, not a sound

I can still hear the marching feet
as I gaze towards the square
and try to place the NAAFI
which was somewhere over there

I can hear the airmen laughing
standing in the cookhouse queue
with berets tucked into their tabs
a vibrant sea of blue

A D.I. would come marching by
and shout loudly in your ear
"get yer bleedin air cut lad"
and report to me back ere

I can hear the PTI's
as they put you through your paces
arms stretch, bend your knees
and cross country blinking races

The bullshit as you clean your huts
the bumper on the floor
the pads you walk with on your feet
the job sheet on the door

Inspections by the officer
you saw from time to time
white glove scraping on the lockers
for the slightest hint of grime

the wash house in the morning frost
you shiver as you shave the fluff
and soap your face with erasmus sticks
or some other shaving stuff

"Stand by your beds" somebody shouts
"Corporal present" God is here
the scramble as you panic
all those faces white with fear

I recall the bayonet charges
at sacks of straw hitched to a rack
I remember missing once or twice
and landing on my back

I can hear the crack of 303's
as you lay there on the floor
the aching shoulder from the kickback
you don't want to be there anymore

I recall the tetanus injections
administered with skill
then back up on the square
for another hour of drill

It all came back as I wandered
through a place that I knew well
Bridgnorth Recruitment training
The British airman's hell

Yet all those years ago
I still see them plain as day
as they departed after passing out
and went their separate ways

Smart lads as I recall
when they went to catch the train
The DI's standing smiling
They got it all to do again

I still hear the ghostly voices
shouting orders everywhere
the sound of marching airmen
seems to fill the morning air

From all corners they came flocking
carrying brand new kit
to join a million others
and do their little bit

Amen.

Albert Forsyth

The Knock

When I married my soldier
How love makes one forget!
When he marches off to war
My life seems to stop
There are people who fill my day
But when night time comes
All rational thought takes flight

During this silent world
When darkness reigns
Happy people sleep
But peace sadly eludes me
Lying all alone, pleading,
begging, listening, offering
silent prayers like a mantra
Please – don't send the knock
How I fear the knock!

That's my greatest fear
Every little sound
Is like an electric shock
The greatest fear of all
Is the Families' Officer's knock
Seeing the gates of Hades opening
Would make heart stop.

When the TV is on
People see my husband's courage
Does anyone think about me?
Sitting on my own
Watching the clock
Tick tock, tick tock

Roberta Coelho

BOMB WATCH IN ARMAGH
(Foot patrols)

And it's Bomb Watch time again,
Where we walk about with the men,
Where we meet hostile people,
As we pass the church steeple,
And we wonder when it will end.

Armagh is a historic city,
But don't you think it's a pity,
When you walk about,
Whenever you go out,
And see bombed out remains.

The shops the houses and pubs,
And the people who only give snubs,
When you say "hello",
Then it's time to go,
And you wish you could find a friend.

Even the children are bought up to hate,
The everyday soldier who walks past their gate,
They must see that it is wrong,
How much longer will this go on,
Why can't the people see sense!!!

Susan Pullar

MY POEM OF COLOUR

Pink is the colour of flowers blowing in the wind
Red is juicy, tasty cherries from branches on the tree
Blue is the colour of the waves out at sea
Black is the night sky without sparkling stars
Yellow is a ball of golden fire in the sky

Tina-Marie Loveridge (age 10)

An Ode To The Red Tops

The location is Suffield, Alberta
The live exercise is Medman
Where troops of the Rhine rehearse for a fight
In that still, yet colourful land.

Gopher, Bald-Eagle, Goshawk and Cougar
Are some just to mention a few
Of the dangerous hours they spend on the block
Longing for skills to improve.

For them it's nerve racking in the assault
Knowing somewhere, somehow, someone's at fault
Because eager to fight the boys will debuss
Safety is nothing they wish to discuss.

To save a life, heroics are born
"Go to checkfire", they look up and scorn
But it's no' finished yet, there's still the fight through
STOP! STOP! STOP! they all wonder who.

Tragedy is something they've just got to hack
Back on goes their orange vest for another attack.
Do they really have talk travelling back, of the Sinbin?
No! All that can be heard is the sounds of the engines.

Some remf's in the bar take offence, think their joyous
"But openly mourning disnae always become us".
The next day when the remf's behind his wee shitty desk
They're back oot on the prairie riskin' their necks

Yes they're back oot on the block come rain or fair weather
Hopin' the O.C.'s plans will all come together.
With a great sense of achievement they all get a lift
When the template turns green at the end of Rourkes Drift

And if you've played this role, stuck to the rules
Down to the last proviso'r
You'll know just what it is to be
A SAFETY SUPERVISOR.

Vincent Campbell

CRY

it takes a lot to set me off,
and i mean really.
lots,
ma mate turns on me.
thats one.
ma bird thats two
im not righting, write.
who am i mad with
guess who.
but i take a step back,
just to think.
wait everyone thinks iv had a drink. again.
would you if you felt this low.
i think so, i think so
wait i drink so,
not,..........
Now come on who do you think you are Martyn

Someone that needs help.
And this a cry,
so stick with me before please before ,.,.,....,..,,,,.,.,,.,

Martyn

POOL

Where will you be, as my eyes close?
warm sea, take me in.
bubbles, how long are your life spans?
do you live forever?

I'm not of a body,
there's none of me left,
I go for a swim in pools of my tears
and then relax as I'm caught in a net.

Washed onto shore it's cool and alive,
I play with the figures I can see in the sky,
patterns on my retina dance as I blink,
there are descending circles and translucent lines.

Lets play on the grass,
shapeless forms pass,
whispers wither by
and my eyes grow heavy.

No sun or satellite to wave goodbye.
I'm submerged. Outline.

Alexandrine

I DREAMED A DREAM

Last night I dreamed a beautiful dream
That I went for a walk with God,
We strolled along a bright sunbeam
Eating chips and battered cod.

He told me that He loved me,
And said, 'He knew I loved Him too.'
He showed me things I wanted to see
Like how He 'made the sky so blue.'

I asked Him, "how mankind was doing?"
But He didn't answer me,
He wasn't very happy
And that was plain to see.

He told me, 'to be careful,
Along the path of life,'
He said, "don't be resentful,"
And to, 'take care of my wife.'

I asked Him, 'How was Jesus?'
He said, "He will be fine
But his wounds have not yet healed,
Even after all this time."

As we walked along the leafy lane,
I tired, so He carried me,
We then sat down, within the shade,
Of a beautiful old oak tree!

I held His hand so tightly
As He cuddled up to me,
His heart was love and comfort,
So I asked to, 'stay for eternity?'

But He replied that, 'I must go
To carry on with my life,'
And as I woke, from my dream
I snuggled up closely to my wife.

I told her that, 'I loved her,'
She said, 'she loved me too.'
I then felt a glow, deep inside
And I knew that my dream was true.

Peter D Bruffell

KITCHEN

A smell from the kitchen is nothing new
However this one it made you PHEW
It crept in silent as the night
In fact it gave us quite a fright

Open windows to clear the air
But the smell it stayed right there
Move the furniture across the room
Lift the carpet chase the fume

Lift the floor board in the room
Sweep it out with little broom
We didn't know its name was Fred
We've just found out, it's long time dead

All those smells around the house
Coming from A LITTLE MOUSE

David Killelay

BLACK AND WHITE

Through the dust and smoke he rises, to rid him of his foe,
Running on full auto, no need for go, go, go,
Following his orders, right down to the last letter,
From recruit, right through to Cpl, always a real go getter.

Back at home on leave again, back to the peace and quiet,
Shopping trips, school runs, and the next big fat free diet,
Back to abstract normality, with all its warming charms,
Hand in hand, in Country Park, with daughter in his arms.

Incoming mortar, "get your bloody heads down",
Effective fire from everywhere, confusion all around,
No time to think of just, what the next hour or so will bring,
Listening to the thumps of mortar, the rounds on metals ping.

Distraction in the form, of letters on the mat,
No need to clear the area, or to reach out for his gat,
Just an easy morning 5 miler, with ipod in his ears,
Still pushes himself whilst he's on leave, automatic after all
these years.

Different country, different reason, but still the same old drills,
No 5 miler in the morning, just straps and pain killing pills,
Ingrained dirt everywhere, in every open pore,
No knocks or even greetings, "just kick down that bloody
door"

This is the life for so many, that others do not know,
Easy in, is easy out, thus, the ebb and flow,
This is the contrast, as simple as plain as day and night,
As similar as some would say, contrasts as black and white.

Larry Taylor

Funny

So often, when in barracks, delight in fisticuffs and brawls.
And yet, when "In Theatre", they might make you sob
with pride,
To see them band like brothers and be counted side by side.
It's funny how the Army's many Regiments and Corps

God bless the British Army, it's an extraordinary thing,
Capable of miracles, enough to make the angels sing.
But, when you leave the Colours, you can't help feel the loss,
You miss all the upheaval, and you actually "Give a toss."

It's so lonely as a Civvy and when problems multiply,
There are few who want to know you when you feel as you
could cry.
But one day, you meet another chap, an old soldier just
like you;
It doesn't matter what he was, because suddenly, one are two.

Then another and another, and before you know what's what.
You're suddenly at section strength, and all talking Tommy rot!
It feels good to have new "Muckers" – they know what
you're about.
You can talk to them for hours - there's never any doubt.

So, don't go feeling down old chum, chin up, chest out,
look straight.
Just cast around, you'll find a pal, and soon you'll feel just
great!

Robert Jenkins

He Doesn't Mean It

He's shouting again
though it brings him more pain
Far more hurting to him than to me
I try hard not to cry though the tears in my eyes
Make it dreadfully hard to see.

I wish he could see what his screams do to me
As he lashes my ears with his tongue
For I can see clearly that he loves me dearly
And he knows I can't help it – I'm young!

But it's over at last the temper has passed;
He gathers me close and I'm glad
That his hurt inside has finally died
As I love him so much – he's my Dad

Sland

ROYAL BRITISH LEGION

It's Armistice Day in November
And Memories don't seem to fade
Time once more for Remembrance
And the Royal British Legion Parade
With their heads held high and shoulders back
There's a hint of sadness in their eyes
Still smart are these "Yesterday Soldiers"
Tho' they now wear suits and ties
Gone for them are the days of Uniform
The Khaki, The Navy and The Blue
Each served the Queen and the Country
All Britain's good men and true
And as they are called to attention
The Bearers their Standards raise
And march to the Local Memorial
In a silent moment each man prays
Then as one the Group of Bearers
Slowly let their Standards fall
As tho' in a quiet answer
To the lonely Buglers Call
And the familiar words they all remember
"At the going down of the Sun"
The universal words for those that were lost
We remember them , every one
So now it's back to attention
With medals on their chests well displayed
As they march away in grand formation
In the Royal British Legion Parade

Dennis Shrubshall

Sleep

Darkness swirls around my head,
as I lie shaking in my bed.
Too scared to sleep, lest I die
Exhaustion beckons as the night flies by

The dreams have come, the panic too
running from things, on a floor of glue
terror unseen, so scared I'll lose
My only solace lies in booze

Sleep deprivation, do others see?
I stay awake till fatigue can take me
The days are long, a dream-like hell
I long for night, but dread it as well

Sammy

PEARL OF DESPAIR

Pearl of despair
Your tracery spreads slowly
The bitterness of our love

Stephen Hill c.

Saying Goodbye To Daddy

Standing
Looking down on the valley,
Searching for our home,
The rain drizzling and pattering my face,
I huddle to my father,
And he wraps his arm around me.
We stand in silence,
Watching smoke drifting from cottage chimneys.

I feel my father's arm tighten,
And his kiss on my hair,
A tear brims in my eye
And then falls onto the muddy ground
Where my welly boots are planted.
I look up at my father's understanding eyes,
And see that he is close to crying.
He hugs me, we become closer than ever.
He tells me to be brave but it is hard
As my tears cascade freely down my cheeks.
He shall be gone in the morning,
And I shall be wishing that I had gone with him.
I hug him, breathing in his familiar smell, burying my nose
in his coat,
Sniffing, then wiping my nose, embarrassed.
He takes my chin and I stare into his eyes looking
at my reflection,
And then I hug him once more
And I know that this is goodbye,
But he shall come home again.

As we trudge home, I grip his hand,
Never wanting to let go, but I have to.
But I know that I shall hold it again, someday.

My Daddy
Ruth Bourne (age 11)

KITCHENER'S MAN

Chorus:
'Tis the sound of the feet, my boy,
'Tis the sound of the marching feet;
'Tis the sound of the bugle's joy,
'Tis the sound of the drummer's beat,
'Tis the sound of the fifer's toy;
'Tis the sound of the War-Call meet.

They're calling for volunteers,
(but it'll be over for Christmas):
United are playing on Saturday;
and there'll be room for a likely lad,
whose fast with his feet
and hard with his fists.

Chorus.

Kitchener's man, you'll be;
and United on Saturday for me:
with my feet and fists, I'll be a likely lad.
You'll not see me, but Saturday,
and I'll not curse and swear
to the Corporal's yell.

Chorus.

Drill your feet to the bone
and wear your hands raw:
dig your trenches and fill your bags,
scream your hate and stab your bayonet;
and sob with fear - (it could be you).
You'll not see me, but Saturday.

Chorus.

You've gone to the Front,
carrying your kitbags
and singing 'Tipperary':
you'll not see me, but Saturday;
(and it'll be over by Christmas);
and you'll be home then: United.

Chorus.

They're calling for volunteers,
(but it'll be over by Easter)
and United play on Saturday;
and a lad whose quick with his feet
and strong with his shoulder,
will find a place – (there's a likely lad).

Chorus.

But Kitchener's man I'll be,
and no Saturday for me;
called to the Colours:
"You'll make a likely lad,
and curse and swear
to the Corporal's yell."

Chorus.

I've drilled me feet bloody
and worn me hands raw;
I've sobbed with fear
and cried with anger.
I've stabbed yon likely dummy
and dug yon bloody trench.

Chorus.

They're sending us off by boat,
the bait cast with the fishing float.
They're sending us off from the coast,
to keep and to feed someone's boast.
They're sending us off to beat
another Country's petty seat.
They're sending us off to caulk
their seams with lead-tongued talk.

Chorus.

They're sending us off to war,
to tread on the greenery and gore.
They're sending us off to fight,
into the unforgiving night.
They're sending us off with music,
"God Save The Peoples' Pridy Physic."
They're sending us off this 'proud day',
"God help us and save us," we pray.

Chorus.

There'll be no bloody Saturday for me,
we're United now, all bloodless faces;
we likely lads called to the Colours –
now all waiting behind the Front,
cold, wet, muddy and miserable:
"Finished by Easter – (?) – bloody Easter!"

Chorus.

Another Christmas, and it'll all be over,
(but you'll take that with a spit in the wind);
here crouch I, 'three-sheets-to-the-wind',
as legless as any gutter drunkard;

my legs stretched before me,
my lap awash with mud and vomit,
my bottom cooled by red-clotted water.

Chorus.

There'll be no Saturday for me,
nor fight against other likely lads,
and I'll not win against United:
I've a pension for me legs
and a medal to remember 'em by.

'Tis the sound of the feet, my boy,
'Tis the sound of the marching feet;
'Tis the sound of the bugle's joy,
'Tis the sound of the drummer's beat,
'Tis the sound of the fifer's toy;
'Tis the sound of the War-Call meet.

And me? I was Kitchener's Man.

*I wrote this in remembrance of my grandfather Harry Clarke who joined the
1st Battalion Royal Warwickshire Regiment in 1913 and went out with
the British Expeditionary Force in that year. He joined as a private, was
wounded in 1916 (rank then was sergeant), at the First Battle of the Somme,
he was promoted to second lieutenant and returned to the front for the second
Battle of the Somme. At the end of the war, he took command of a Chinese
Labour Battalion that was doing battlefield clearance on the Somme. He
married Anne Weaver whose health was affected by their living on the Somme
(most of which was a marsh), and in 1922 he resigned his commission
(captain) to look after his wife. He was a gentle man and I remember him
with much love. I wrote this around the time of the Falkland's War. It should
be read at a speed of 120 paces per minute.*

WE SHALL BE STRONG

Slowly the train chugged away
Slowly moving day by day

I dare not cry
I know someone out there will die

I had my Teddy in my arm
We're going to stay on a farm

"Good-bye Mum" I say quietly
Are we really going to be 'Evacuees'?

After six years we return home
For a second I think I'll be left alone

Suddenly I hear my name
"Mummy, Daddy, we're home again"

Emma Deborah Schmittner (age 12)

Another Mans War!

My baby's all grown up now, and fighting another mans war
Although still a child himself, he's on an Iraqi tour
I can't explain my feelings of helplessness and despair
My need to hold and hug you, and show you that I care

My thoughts are always with you, I've shed a silent tear
That you're kept safe from harm, and soon be back home here
My hearts overwhelmed with pride, of the person you've become
You're achieving your goals; I am the proudest Mum.
I know the Army's your family for now, and you're watching each others backs
I hope that is enough for you, and not just papering over cracks.

Your young eyes will see sorrow, hate, despair, and pain.
Keep true to yourself son, and let your dignity remain.
When it's all over, and your back home safe and well
My shoulders are here to lean on, what ever you wish to tell.

Alison Mitchell

GRANDDAD

A frail old man with warmth around him,
A smile on his face, his family surround him.
'Oh Danny Boy' he sings with a glint in his eye,
Teaching me domino's as the time goes by.

You didn't tell me granddad of your memories past,
Of when you walked strong in days gone fast,
I never knew of your days at war,
Barbed wire, the sandy beaches wore.

Marching onto the 'Orion' at Liverpool Docks,
Days and nights at sea, forever went the clocks.
Arriving in the mystic east, disembarking in Bombay,
On a train to Bangalore, in a basha you had to stay.

You never told me granddad of your birthday in Madras,
Drinking local fire water, how you had a blast.
Moving to Thailand to bathe in hot springs,
Wondering in the Jungle such amazing things.

All I have now Granddad are your memories on paper,
You'll never be forgotten, we will always remember.

Lisa Robinson

HIGH SOCIETY DREAMER

Walking, with medals on his chest
A man of no fixed abode
"He's a tramp," I heard someone say
"Just an old man of the road."
Yet he's a high society dreamer
Years ago he did what he could,
Now he can't forget the memories
Of the shedding of all that blood.

Little lad sits on his doorstep
No shoes upon his feet,
From a single parent family
With barely enough to eat.
Though he's a high society dreamer
Dreaming of the day
When he and many like him
Can stand and have their say.

Young woman on street corners
Her miniskirt short and red
It's the only thing she knows
Her living made on a bed.
But she's a high society dreamer
Dreaming about the time
She doesn't have to sell herself
By living this life of crime.

So listen you politicians
And you Whitehall men,
Stop thinking only of yourself,
Try to think of them.
Those high society dreamers
The one's that dream and scheme,
And when you go to bed tonight
Have a low society dream.

John A Silkstone

SCARED

I'm scared I'll never see you again,
That you'll leave me all alone.
I need you in my life,
For you are my guiding star.

I'm scared you'll leave without,
Saying goodbye.
That I'll say something hurtful,
And you'll go away disappointed.

I'm scared I'll fail,
Your understanding,
Your trust,
Your hopes in me.

I'm scared I'll,
Lose you forever,
And I'll never hold you close,
Or tell you that I love you again.

Kayleigh Carey

Whispers In My Mind

As I read and as I listen to what's written and what's said,
Through all the words and pictures come the voices of the dead.
When I see commemorations, all my comrades row on row
The voices swirl and whisper as they speak from long ago.

"If we fill your recollections, if you hear us in your head
Then our spirits live forever, though our bodies are long dead.
Though the reasons that we went to war, the reasons we
were slain,
May be lost – we're not forgotten so our deaths were not in vain."

When I stop before the tablet where the names are carved in stone,
Though I'm standing solitary, suddenly I'm not alone.
As the wind tugs at my blazer, and a tear forms in my eye,
I hear the voices murmur on the breeze's rising sigh.

"If we fill your waking moments, if we haunt you when you dream,
If recalling us brings anguish and the pain becomes extreme,
Just remember we were brothers once and will be once again
You've not forgotten us and so our deaths were not in vain."

So I march with all my comrades and we tread the well-worn route
As our band of close-knit brothers heads towards the last salute.
But the whispering voices echo and I can't ignore their call
For the one voice speaks for many and the many speak for all.

"If we fill your final moments when at last you come to rest,
If the memories you had of us were always at our best,
If you kept us in your soul with no surrender to the pain,
Then we've always been beside you, and our deaths were not
in vain."

Brian Keith Bilverstone

The Eyes Of A Child

Can you see the horror in her dark brown eyes
Can you smell the charred flesh?
Can you hear the cries?
This child has seen the bloodshed
This child can survive
Her eyes have dried of tears now
Yet this child is only Five!

Bosnia Christmas 1996.
Derek Blackburn

A Promise Is A Promise

The letter came and I wondered what to say
As I held it in my hands
As his father had made a promise to return to him that day

I walked into his bedroom and I turned to him and said
"My darling Daddy's not coming home" and he looked up
from his bed

"I know that Daddy's not coming home to stay here anymore
He stopped to see on his way to heaven just once more
He said he'd promised to see me when he got back
And a promise is a promise he told me flat

"I'll love you till the stars fall out the sky
And tell your Mom I love her, but I know she'll cry
I love you both and I'll see you when you're done
And when you're up in heaven to the pearly gates I'll run
And we'll be together just you wait and see
Because you are the sun and moon to me"

Then Daddy left and gave me this for you"
I looked down at my son's tiny hand and knew
For in it was a clip on which flew butterflies
And straight away the tears cam to my eyes

I cried because I knew he told the truth
Because I'd given it to his father before he'd joined his troop
And felt that all my happiness had gone
On that terrible day during the storm

I held the clip in my hands once more
Then kissed my child and walked out of the door
I put the clip into my hair as old
And I knew my husband was okay once more
Because he'd kept a promise to show us both
That we meant the most to him no matter what

Anne-Marie Spittle   89

JOSIE'S FIRST DAY

I awaken at 6:00 a.m.
To a beautiful, warm October day
I take a warm bath
And pray that I can find my way.

The pain is very mild
All I can think……..
I might wait a while.

As the hours pass on
The pain gets stronger
Time to go to the hospital
I can't wait any longer.

The nurse asked me,
"Can you make it to labor and Delivery?"
I told her that I can walk and do this on my own
With my hands trembling and my body shivering.

They came in to check me
Started screaming and yelling
"Call the doctor right now!"
"This baby is coming."

I was 5 ½ centimeters
It may be a little longer
Lord help me Jesus
These contractions are even stronger!

Within 45 minutes
Her head was crowning
I pushed and pushed and pushed
And felt is if I were drowning.

The doctor came in
With only one glove on
To catch this baby
Who had waited so long.

As she enters this life
She doesn't even know
What lies ahead of her
Or how much she'll grow.

This beautiful little girl is all mine
Her cheeks are all rosy
And today is her day...............
This is Josie!

Christie Bowman
From Missouri

No Matter The Years

A part of time and our hearts stopped at that
moment that no matter how many years pass will
feel like yesterday. The memory of the knock on the door,
seeing two class A uniforms in the glow
of the porch light, the turn of our color to paste
from the message sent by the Secretary of the Army,
that anchor that dragged us into the darkness of an ocean deep
where we fought for oxygen, fought to shed
the weight of why, fought to care for ourselves,
fought to reach the surface and carry forth your legacy.

It's been written that with death a spouse loses their partner,
a child loses a parent, but parents lose their future.

Now four years later
the surprising part is that the burden delivered
to our souls that day didn't kill us. That it
has lightened and the tears don't fall
as often although we're still not sure we've accepted
that you are anyplace else except travelling
the globe with your surfboard, gliding on your snowboard
down mountains that touch the sky, shadowing
quietly behind each of us who loved you,
letting us see and feel you through a heart shaped
leaf on the walkway at our door, the kiss of a breeze across
our face, or the hawk that still calls often from the oak.
Or that you remain ever so quietly still clutching your motto
Toujours Pret, Always Ready,
still covering and protecting your brothers
still suffering the desert sands.

For our son Patrick 8/25/70 – 2/11/04
Deb Tainsh, Georgia, USA. Wife of US Marine Corps (28yrs, ret'd 1994)
Sgt Major. Proud mom of Sgt Patrick Tainsh, KIA 2/11/04 Baghdad,
Bronze & Silver Star recipient.

CLOUDS

As children we love to watch the clouds
They drift majestically by
Their power and force we watch in awe
As seen through a youngsters eyes.

As adults we don't notice clouds
Their presences no longer thrill
We have no time to see god's gift
No time to just stand still.

Our minds are clouds
We don't have need
To think of worlds apart
The only clouds that we now see
Is when life is torn apart?

These clouds are seen through ransacked lands
Created by man's own greed
Produced by the fanatic's misguided hands
Where hatred can quickly breed.

Our children still want to watch the clouds
Let's hope the world will learn
The type of clouds that we must see
Don't maim & kill & burn.

A B Jones

Forgive Me Brother

Forgive me brother
For I do not cry upon the world's shoulders
I do not mourn upon thy death
I do not seek sympathy from those unknown
But I expect your memory to maintain and withhold
In the world's structure when I grow old.

As time may go
And age may sweep upon me
I shan't forget your face
nor the memories which were brought

As time increased and paths were led
I shan't forget the pain and tears which I shed
Behind this face lies the truth
Of all which was to be said and all which is still within
My heart break shall stay inside me

Forgive me brother
If I do not visit your graveside
If I do not pledge my grief
By the growing grass
Near your stone or side
If I do not claim my love

Forgive me brother
For I am hiding
Form the world
Which seems
So impure
But which once seemed
Clear and defiant
When you walked in a room.

Forgive me brother
I am unclear
Unsure
Of where this world is leading me
Promise you will guide me
I shan't forget thee.

Ruth Rayment

FOR DAD

You gave me life
You nurtured me
You taught me right from wrong
You instilled in me a love of life
And taught me to be strong;
To face whatever life threw at me
Head on, don't run away.
But you've gone now from this life
And I miss you every day

I am so proud to be your daughter, dad
But it's hard to be strong when you're hurting
When everything reminds me of you
Perhaps one day I'll smile again
I know you'd want me too
You know I was a daddy's girl
You were the first love of my life
So sleep safely my adored daddy

Till we meet again

For my dad, who died very suddenly in September 07
Jane mac

First Days

You will be the Smartest!
You will be the toughest!
You will be the fittest!
You will be the best by far!!

Shining Parades!
Spit and Polish!
Bedding Blocks!
Regimental History!

Trained Soldiers!
L/SGT Squad Instructor!
GOLD SGT Platoon Boss!
R.S.M. GOD!!!!!!!!!!

Write home phone home.
Trips to the N.A.F.F.I.
Running, every day.
Drill even in your sleep.

Long days short nights.
Get out of bed.
Hands off cocks onto socks.
Swing those arms on the way to Scoff.

FIRST DAYS!!!!!!!!!!!!!!!!!!!

Nick Taylor

The Moon Your Mirror

I will hold you up to the night
The moon your mirror
The sky is black
Youthful dreams a tear away
I hold you tight
Under no illusions
I won't speak out loud
Or out of thought
I will please you
And your smile will take me through
The coldness of the night.

I once heard of the dying wish
A wishing well for old desires
It never happened me
But your eyes will open the heart
Hypnotise the myth
And when you do
I will be there to feel
Feel the warmth grow inside you again.

I will hold you up to the night
My love for you will keep my eyes from closing
And my envy will shine like the summer sun
And I will feel happy
I will hold you up to the night
And hope your calling will chance
Oh how I wish for chance to smile on you
A wish I would happily die for.

I will hold you up to the night
Under shining stars I will pray
Under shinning stars I will wonder
My love
My angel
I will never leave you
And if need be
I shall hold you forever
Up to the night
The moon as your mirror.

Morrison 1976

BELIEVE
Lyrics to a song I wrote

I stepped outside the sky was all torn this sad old town just
waiting to fall
It's not the way we planned it to be
Like plastic soldiers left out on the wall shoulder to shoulder
and waiting to fall

We flew the flag of red black and blue and built a tank from
paper and glue
And went to war for something to do
Playing at soldiers we hid in the sand eagerly awaiting our
next command

Standing in line just frozen in time
You've got to play the game, got mud on your face its your
turn to hide..
We almost had it all you've got to believe
That forever we are heroes, you've got to believe

You played outside with your gang and me and ran home
scared in time for your tea
It's not the way that warfare should be
But then we weren't soldiers our backs to the wall shoulder
to shoulder and waiting to fall

Standing in line just frozen in time
You've got to play the game, got blood on your face its your
turn to die..
We almost had it all you've got to believe
That forever we are heroes, you've got to believe

Bang bang you stand in line you gotta wait around for re supply

Bang bang they shot you down you gonna be leaving this old town

Bang bang too young to die you had no time to say good bye

Bang bang the battles won too many lost an only son

Will Kevans

Poppy
WWI

Barley and rye sway in the breeze no more
A poppy stands tall – alone – a monument in this field
of misery.
Where a soldier fell in the Great War
Scarlet petals now bask in the golden rays of sun,
Soaking up the glory of the summer's day;
No more fighting where the soldiers lay.
Clouds gather and darkness reigns
Soft tears of the gods fall gently on the land
Renewing life, creating new birth:
Seeds sprout on the dawn of a new peace.

The fields are silent now and all have gone home,
Except for those who lie beneath the scarlet petals:
Whatever their names – whichever side they belong to-
They will never go home though never will be forgotten.
For they are a symbol of new life - of new hope - a scarlet
poppy:
A reminder of that terrible war

Slowly the seeds come back and the seasons pass
Barley and rye sway in the breeze once more
Yet through it all a monument still stands tall -
A row of scarlet poppies
A testament to those awful years
Let's remember them all as we watch the poppies sway
In the warm summers breeze – a scarlet symbol of new hope

Andy Cook

A Special Friend

It is to you, this message I send,
Thank you, for being my friend.
I wouldn't have you any other way,
You always have kind words to say.
When im down and feeling blue,
The one to cheer me up is you.
Always there when I need you, you're never far,
A special friend, that you are.
In times of sorrow, you lend a hand,
You always seem to understand.
You're always honest, always true,
There's no other friend I have like you.
You always call me on the phone,
And leave a message if im not home.
We have great fun when were together,
I want us to be friends forever.
It's nice to have a friend that cares,
It's nice to have a friend that shares.
All I have, to you I would give,
My friend it's you, I love to be with.

Tina Howarth

Can't sleep, afraid to dream
Can't wake, too tired for lack of sleep
Can't love for fear of losing
Losing you because I can no longer love

Days turned upside down
No focus, no structure
Time disappears without recollection
I plan so much, but achieve so little

Ironclad exterior, jelly at the core
The mask is all that binds me
I struggle to mouth the truth
Do you really want to hear my story?

Crying in my dreams, transported back to '82
The gorse and peat are still burning
Lanolin, smoke and cordite
The smells offend my nostrils

Every year I'm carried back, an eternal bond
Goose Green, a brief but violent visit
Yet vivid in my thoughts
Do they think of me, as I of them?

I lost it once in '85, it only cost my marriage
A minimal price some would say, a glitch
An aberration, that's life, it happens!
Replaced the lid and carried on

I have a life, but not worth living
Invasive thoughts of death
A simple task to end it all
A struggle to maintain control

Feelings of dysfunction
Arms and legs, diminished feeling
Pain radiating throughout a ravaged body
Saddened eyes holding back tears

I could cry, but would anyone hear me
I will not show my weakness
A sense of pride holds me tight
Duty refuses to give up

The second time was '95
I thought the end was due
But no, I found the lid once more
Renewed the armour against the world

Then, alcohol induced psychosis
A comfortable friend
Long nights without reality
An empty, numb existence

In '02 life became a blur
A mystic fusion of realities
Raging heartbeat in my ears
Control, a seldom luxury

Struggle to maintain reality
A desire to own my fears
Fear of owning anything at all
Life without an existential meaning

If I cried, you'd see me bared
Undressed and naked as a child
I want to share my feelings
But would you survive the deluge?

I am tired, middle aged and marking time
A half lived post war dream
Years fit snugly into thoughts
A lifetime translated into moments

Now the final bureaucratic humiliation
An intimate inquisition, irrefutable proof of life
Ill and tired of repetition, I want to rest
To be finished, 25 years on

Graham Cordwell

A HERO SOLDIER

In Basra's war torn city, a soldier stands so tall,
Smiling at the locals, with his back against a wall,
Beneath a veil of calmness, his heart beats like a drum,
Thinking of the folks he loves, his girl back home and Mum,

The sun is burning down on him, it burns his reddened skin,
This checkpoint duty daily, wears his temper wafer thin,
Another hour of waiting, to protect this peasant mob
Then back home to the bunker for a shower and get
some grub

A young girl reaches up to him, a scar upon her face,
Her Daddy won't be coming home, this picture takes his place,
A tear runs down a dirty cheek and rags adorn her feet,
She laughs then skips to join the queue for bread and food
to eat,

A cloud of dust arises, a scream runs through the stalls,
His senses into overdrive, he strains to see the cause,
He sights a dark Sedan, inside a body dressed in black,
The soldier charges forward screaming warnings to get back,

He clearly sees the face and eyes of one that's set to die,
His forward movement halted, as he hears a muted cry,
The girl that smiled so kindly now lay injured on the ground,
He stoops to raise her fragile form, and turns himself around

The blast was heard for miles around, he felt the red hot air,
Felt molten iron down his back; his head was raised in prayer,
God help this tiny child I hold, the last thought in his mind,
His limbs were scattered far and wide, the pieces all to find

Quiet through the market now, the dust cloud fell to ground,
A mourning mass was gathered, such a grisly mess they found
The soldiers body buried deep beneath a market stall,
A muffled cry of help they heard, a tiny little call

They dug and pulled the stall out, the soldier long was dead,
But underneath his body they could see a tiny head,
They lifted out the torso, and then helped her stand alone
She could not see the carnage yet or hear the injured moan

In Basra's war torn city, a soldier stands so tall,
Smiling at the locals, with his back against a wall,
He wonders who the plaque was for fifteen years ago
A scarred girl lays her flowers, says a prayer and turns to go

Mick Heywood

A Proud Corps?

From the tender age of two it became apparent what I would
eventually do.
So many photographs, black and white and slide, my future
they could not hide.
Stood to attention, proud and erect, saluting to so my respect.
As early as age would allow, uniform and discipline became
my vow.

The age I don't remember, but the Scouts found
a new member.
Naïve and tender I may have been, but this was the start of the
future I'd seen.
Army Cadets were yet to come, but now I could see what
needed to be done.
Academics required by law, were only needed to join
the Corps.

1982 became the year, the earliest I could be a Royal Engineer.
The first modern war, with Journalists, live satellite pictures
and more.
Had recently been won, by an Army of which I was now one.
8000 miles, beers and laughs, to remove the Argies
from the Malvinas.

Time for me was clearly set, 22 years, a challenge to be met.
Doubtless the work would be hard, as it had been for Lt Chard.
But from the training I did not shirk, the threat was there and
so was the work.
Many hours all year round, spent training in the life
I had found.

The years rolled by, and half the world I saw with my own eye.
Often working from dawn still 'til night, but always feeling
that this was right.
The work was always at a max, but as Engineers we knew how
to relax.
No matter where we'd be, so was to bar, and with Squadron
funds, often free.

But alas this could last, a strong Army was a thing of the past.
The politicians in Whitehall, decided the nineties the time
to call.
Years of experience to be gone, 3 stages of management lost
as one.
This left gaps that had to be filled, mainly with yes men, and
the weak willed.

Fortunately some did escape the net, but now commitment
could not be met.
Three times the work for a third of the strength, just made
tours of a greater length.
More often we went away, and with many a marriage went
astray.
But still we stayed for the fun, our mates and to work as one.

Now it has become horribly clear, the price of redundancy
was far too dear.
The yes men now in power, force the fun to hide and cower.
A modern Army we may be, but the state of morale is not
down to me.
They say the old sweats spread dissension, but that's just their
mis-comprehension.

If the likes of me and my kind, feel it's time for a new life
to find
The reason for the roam. Is much deeper than the odd moan.
Our discomfort with our lot, is not the start of a declining rot.
It's too late for that, it has begun, and the pace is fast becoming
a run.

Many with the knowledge to know better, are now asking for
their letter.
This Corps has changed beyond belief, and getting out the
only relief.
It's come to this sad day, when the only thing left to say,
Is that those who control a Corps so proud, are more interested
in men that follow the crowd!!

Wayne Shenton

ANOTHER YEAR WASTED

Another year spent, another year wasted.
Another year kept, from the joys I could've tasted.

Another year spent, for those disappointed in me.
Another year spent, being the person i'm NOT supposed
to be.

All the hopes and dreams I had for the years ahead,
Are now distant memories, filled with sorrow and dread.

I once had a plan, I had my life on track.
Now I just wish, I could have those years back.

I can once remember a time, before the heartbreak
and the drugs.
A time filled with trust, many kisses, and hugs.

I have caused so much worry, heartache and pain.
Often times I wonder if things could ever be the same.

I not only hurt myself, I hurt those who care.
Many people don't realize, the heavy cross I bear.

All the goals I had for the future, have come and gone away.
The pain of failure haunts me, each and every day.

I fear I've lost control, of the life I once had.
I never would've dreamed, things would ever get this bad.

Drugs have taken from me, my home, my car, and my wife.
The pain these drugs have caused me, cuts me like a knife.

My life has been filled with heartache, many drugs, and hell.
Now I find myself struggling, just to stay away from jail.

I'm not so happy now, I havent been in years.
When I stop to think about it, I can't control my tears.

I've tasted true love, only once in my life.
I thought she was the one, so I made her my wife.

It seems I chose poorly, for she was'nt the one.
I woke up one morning, and sadly she was gone.

I've had my heart mistreated, cheated on, and broken.
Wondering what words I should've said, but often left
unspoken.

A broken heart cannot be fixed with regret, time, or glue.
Only healed by another love, who's faithful, kind, and true.

Everyone I love, seems to go away
Leaving my life empty, at least for today.

Mikael Hall

Where Is He?

Deep in my sleep at night I think I've seen him there,
walking on the hill with the rain drops in his hair.
Down by the garden wall or by the tractor shed,
I know I've seen him somewhere here inside my head.

Over by the burn today I'm sure I saw him pass,
or was it him I thought I saw sitting on the grass.
I thought I heard his voice today from the room next door,
or was it just the whisper of the breeze upon the floor.

Now and then I'll find myself thinking on my own,
and find it hard to understand why I feel so all alone.
And then I think of Donald and how he was with us,
and know he wouldn't want to be the cause of all this fuss.

All this time I've looked for him and haven't found him yet,
I've looked in all those places I thought he liked the best.
I think I'll pop down to the church to pray and talk a while,
and ask the Lord to walk with us along this lonely mile.

Lord I am not worthy but help me please this day,
to let me understand the reason Donald couldn't stay.
As night descends and wraps us up we turn our thoughts to
you,
we offer up our prayers and now a kiss for Donald too.

Dear Lord I have been foolish to look elsewhere but here,
I should have looked here sooner and saved myself a tear.
As soon as I walked in just now I saw him sitting there,
close by your side for ever more we place him in your care.

Written in memory of Donald Blackburn

Peter John Macdonald

114

CHRISTMAS

It's Christmas here in Afrika,
But you wouldn't really know,
There is no old time festive spirit,
With no chance of any snow,

As night falls I see them gather around the fire,
They are strangely not so full of woe and need,
I eye these troops I've trained and pushed,
And indeed they are a special breed,

Darkened, shiny faces all,
With great big widening grins,
Teeth as white as any glistening snow,
As they start to hum their hymns,

Soon clapping, laughing, dancing too,
Spontaneously break out,
I've no idea what they sing now,
But it's happy so I too clap and shout,

I'm dragged up off my chair like log,
And forced to dance their jig,
I make a mess, I feel a fool,
But cheers and claps are what they give,

Such hardship these men have known,
Their sorrow caused by hostilities,
Husbands, wives and children lost,
But still they manage to smile with glee,

I know someday I'll leave these men,
And will have to say my goodbyes,
Their families with such strong bonds,
Just thinking of this fills my eyes,

Twice I've come, and twice I've gone,
And many friends I've lost along the way,
But I know that this last time that I went,
Would be the last time I would ever stay,

Many years have passed, since those days,
But each year in late December,
I raise my glass each Christmas day,
My private toast, as I remember.

(1987 – 2007)
James 2W

CHRISTMAS AT WAR

Here's to the soldier
On Christmas Eve
Alone, by himself –
Not granted leave.

There's no letting up
for Yule-tide you know
The battles go on
Against the foe.

There's a war to be won
And someone must fight
All through the day
And into the night.

In England the family
Have turkey and trifle
While the soldier aims
Then fires his rifle.

The shooting continues
And many are hit.
Wounded and dying
They continue with grit.

The children at home
Have presents to open
While on the battlefield
Old wounds reopen.

Without a break
The battles went on
The cannons kept firing
Until we won.

The News goes home
Of those who died
But kept on fighting
With burning pride.

The baby who never
Knew his dad
Has grown into
A little lad.

The mother alone
Who must carry on,
Without a husband
Has not won.

Someone, Somewhere,
Will always want more
There will always be
One more war.

Jennifer Hyslop

The Single Soldier's Kind of Christmas.

We turned a locker on its side,
To make a kind of bar.
And Smudger cut some tinfoil out,
To make a kind of star.

Then Oscar took a woodland stroll,
To find a kind of tree.
When asked how much it cost replied,
"To you? It's kind of free."

Old Chalkie's Frau made Stollen brot,
A kind of German pud.
Another pad sent sausage rolls,
Which tasted kind of good.

But other skills were needed now,
For a special kind of task,
To find that golden liquid treat,
In a pressured kind of cask.

This task fell on to Shifty Cobb,
A crafty kind of chap,
He came back with Rhineland wine,
Quite cheap but kind of crap.

And so we sent for Lofty Len,
Who was really kind of small.
He trotted off to Paderborn,
To a kind of Brauerei hall.

Then Lofty came back grinning wide,
And got a kind of cheer.
For with him came ten cases of
A special kind of beer.

So, well supplied with drinks and food,
All I can kind of say;
A rare auld time was had by all,
That kind of Christmas Day.

Paddy Slevin

OUR HEARTS AND MINDS

In a place some call the "Emerald Isle,"
for the past year or two has been home.
I'd never have guessed the effect it would have
on a man with a heart made of stone.

I knew not a thing of "the troubles" out here,
but I learnt as my life trickled by.
The country so fine and its people so warm,
sure this "war" it was surely a lie.

Of all of the folk that live here in this land,
just a few are enough to cause strife.
And to make themselves heard and force us to hear,
they've made themselves God and take life.

Some good people stood and said what they thought,
they raised up their doves made of card.
But those men without faces just mocked what they did,
and continued to fill the graveyards.

The political people from this side and that,
they spoke, promised, turned and condemned.
But the one thing they all could agree without doubt,
was this peace that's been broken must mend.

So here we are now and my son's turning ten,
and my daughter she's just become eight.
And it hurts in my heart to watch them grow up,
in this land that's torn up with such hate.

I watch them at night as they watch the TV,
and they hear about murders and all.
And it's now I realise that to give them a chance,
it's off we must be job and all.

I don't want to leave this place I call home
but I know what I do must be done.
I sit in my porch as the night wraps us up,
watching dreams fade and sink with the sun.

So we've packed up our bags and we're leaving at last,
this most beautiful country we love.
And I hope with my all that the peace does return,
and you'll no longer need your white doves.

My thanks for your time and may your God bless you all,
may the peace that you search for come through.
For understand this if you don't find it soon,
even God may give up and go too!

Murdock
Just a soldier

Thinking of You Thinking of Me

When you are laughing, I will feel happy for you
When you are crying I shall cry too
The tears of pain are felt within all
So no need for you my name to call
For within an instant, I shall be at your side
So wipe away those tears you have cried
The thread of one's life is very thin
The consciousness of your soul dwells within
The very fabric of your being
Is never knowing or never seeing
With faith in the saviour we can overcome
The pains of life when life is done
Many have gone before me; I did not pave the way
The lord held out his hand as I heard him say
Your soul was my church; your thoughts were my decree
I am your shepherd and you have followed me.
Now to greener pastures leaving sadness and pain
Knowing that my love shall always remain
Close to those that I have left behind
Praying memories of good times will stay in their mind
We shall meet again, wait and see
Thinking of you thinking of me.

Mark Wiggins

THE FACE

The whistle blew and, veiled in a dense cloud of smoke,
the train pulled out on its long journey to the battlefields
A face caught my eye, the face of a young man barely out of
adolescence,
His thin, pale face shadowed by the sombre khaki of his
feather-trimmed hat
His eyes dark, looking not outward at the summer sunshine,
but toward the deep chasm of the unknown

It was not a time for laughter and gaiety – the news was
trickling through
Brought by letters to loved ones
Trumpeted in newspaper articles
And made real by the slowly growing tide of human debris
spat out of the uncaring,
omnivorous jaws of war

What were these boys going to?
What dark thoughts enveloped them as they went
willingly to defend a home, a country, a way of life?
Would it be worth the speeches, the toasts, the proud bearings
of family and friends,
the shy glances of young girls seeing only the dashing
uniform, and nothing of the
frightened soul beneath

Would the flame of patriotism burn brighter in the trenches,
or would it be quenched,
maybe forever, by the flash of maxim and mortar.............

Just for a moment our eyes met, and for an instant we looked
into each other's soul –
the carefree civilian and the young soldier
And as I turned for home, fighting my own battle against the
public spirit of
patriotism, I wondered,
What would my thoughts and feelings be
If that soldier was me?

Judith Schofield
Military Education
CSIC CNNSW

The Long Awaited Night

Tears fell down her cheeks, caressing her face
as she read the old letters outlined in lace.
Edges are yellow from years gone by,
as the letters she wrote always made her cry.

These letters are some that could never be sent,
for they were written for her marine husband Kent.
He'd gone away to war so long ago,
how long would he be gone – she didn't know.

A prisoner of war, he'd ended up to be,
and her husband, she knew, she would never again see.
Ten years had passed since that awful news,
but to give up on him, she would always refuse.

Alone in her bed she hugged his pillow,
and thought of him, her knight, her hero.
Her dreams are of times so distant and far,
Kent had always been, and will be her star.

Awakened from her sleep by a rap on the door,
she sleepily rose and was chilled to the core.
Rubbing her shoulders, she warmed herself
then picked up the hair pin that lay on the shelf.

With hairpin in place, she decided to walk
to the front door to see who wanted to talk..
When she opened the door, she gasped in surprise,
and a single tear fell from each of her eyes.

For the man before her was much older now,
but to her, he still looked younger somehow.
He said no words, but leaned on his crutch,
and reached for the woman he loved so much.

They found peace in their embrace, and were now complete,
these two that were separated; and time couldn't defeat.
Instead of the pillow to hug that night,
she hugged her hero, her long awaited knight.

Heidi L Cristman

A Single Poppy

Single Poppy standing still
You grow because man will kill
Your colour represents the dead
The blood they lost becomes your red
You bow your head and give a nod
Another life you give to god.

Wendy Shone